Nine Big Easter Eggs

Marjorie Angela Murray

AuthorHouse™
1663 Liberty Drive
Bloomington, IN 47403
www.authorhouse.com
Phone: 833-262-8899

Because of the dynamic nature of the Internet, any web addresses or links contained in this book may have changed since publication and may no longer be valid. The views expressed in this work are solely those of the author and do not necessarily reflect the views of the publisher, and the publisher hereby disclaims any responsibility for them.

This book is printed on acid-free paper.

ISBN: 978-1-4259-1559-9 (sc)

Print information available on the last page.

Published by AuthorHouse 02/27/2024

authorHOUSE

DEDICATED TO :

MY SON MARK E MURRAY
AND
MY FIRST GRAND DAUGHTER
SHANIYA D MURRAY.

IT WAS A BRIGHT AND SUNNY DAY.

WHEN SUE AND MARK WENT OUT TO PLAY.

LOOKING FOR THOSE NINE BIG EASTER EGGS, MAMA HAD HIDDEN AWAY.

MAMA CAME TO THE WINDOW. HELLO SUE AND MARK.

IT'S TIME TO GO HUNTING FOR YOUR NINE BIG EASTER EGGS.

OK MAMA, SAID THE CHILDREN, AND OFF THEY RAN THROUGH THE FIELD.

SUE FOUND THE FIRST BIG EASTER EGG. WHAT COLOR IS IT SHOUT MAMA?

YELLOW SUE SHOUT BACK, AS SUE AND MARK WALK THROUGH THE BEAUTIFUL FLOWER PATCH.

TRY NOT   TO MISS FINDING THOSE BIG EGGS , MAMA SAID, O MAMA, CRY SUE

I'VE FOUND THE SECOND BIGGEST EGG. WHAT COLOR IS IT? SAID MAMA. GREEN SUE SHOUT BACK, MY FAVORITE COLOR.

MARK WAS GETTING FRUSTRATED BUT HE KEPT
WALKING. O MAMA CRY MARK

I'VE FOUND THE BIGGEST EGG OF ALL. WHAT COLOR IS IT
SHOUT MAMA? PURPLE.

SUE AND MARK'S SURPRISE WAS HID IN THE BIG PURPLE EGG. OPEN THAT BIG EASTER EGG AND TELL ME WHAT YOU SEE.

MAMA, MAMA CRY MARK.

THERE ARE FIVE EGGS INSIDE THE PURPLE EGG.

THERE IS ONE MORE BIG EASTER EGG TO BE FOUND. AND I MUST FIND IT SAID MARK. MARK THOUGHT OF SINGING A SONG. SUE CAN WE SING TOGETHER?

COME TO ME BIG EASTER EGG AND I WILL BE YOUR FRIEND. OK SAID SUE AND OFF THEY RAN.

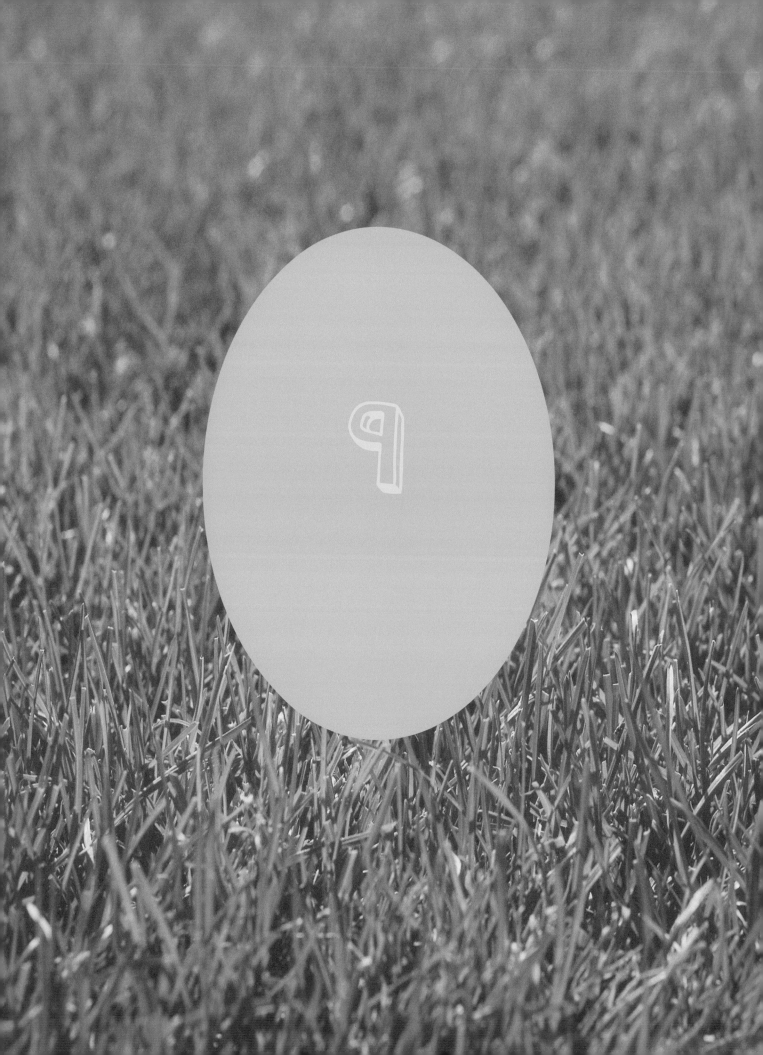

Printed in the United States
by Baker & Taylor Publisher Services